IMAGES
of England
ALONG
THE
RIVER DART

Revd Perry Keene, Grand National Archery Champion, 1898. The clergyman was the vicar of Dean Prior, a village in the heart of Dartmoor near the West Dart, which was owned by the Giles family of Bowden in the parish of Ashprington and Totnes. The Tudor mansions, Bowden House and Dean Court, were built by John Giles, the richest man in Devon. His son, Edward, was knighted in 1604 in recognition of his distinguished military career. Another famous soldier from the area, Colour Sergeant John Prettyjohn, won the Victoria Cross during the Crimean War. He had earlier displayed great courage as a boy at Dean Combe, when he pursued a robber across the moor, successfully apprehending the villain at Hexworthy!

IMAGES
of England

ALONG
THE
RIVER DART

Compiled by
Mike Holgate

TEMPUS

First published 1999
Copyright © Mike Holgate, 1999

Tempus Publishing Limited
The Mill, Brimscombe Port,
Stroud, Gloucestershire, GL5 2QG

ISBN 0 7524 1561 1

Typesetting and origination by
Tempus Publishing Limited
Printed in Great Britain by
Midway Clark Printing, Wiltshire

Contents

Robert Cranford produced this map in 1890, for his annual guide *Up and Down the River Dart*. The publisher founded the *Dartmouth Chronicle* in 1854 and was elected Mayor of Dartmouth in 1871. Following his death in 1901, his family continued the business until 1938.

Introduction

From Dartmoor to Dartmouth, the Dart's waters flow from prehistory into history, passing through the many diverse communities along its banks. Before compiling this book, my own observations of the area had been restricted to enjoyable days out visiting numerous enchanting spots along the river – which Queen Victoria once compared to 'the beautiful Rhine'. Therefore, armed with a potted history gleaned from hearing a pleasure-boat skipper's narration during a trip up the Dart, a few dusty reference works and access to the wonderful pictorial record stored at the Local Studies Archive at Torquay Library, diligent research provided a fascinating educational insight into the history of the Dart Valley. It was enlightening to learn that Totnes, established during my lifetime as the post-hippy capital of alternative Britain, was once a major trading centre. Sad to say, it had also escaped my notice that Benedictine monks had laboured for over thirty years this century to build Buckfast Abbey! Hard to believe that Dittisham and Stoke Gabriel, now providing holiday homes for the rich and famous, or havens for the retired, were once occupied by generations of fishermen, or that Galmpton, Dartmouth and Kingswear have a proud tradition of ship-building. Obvious from the start, however, was the fact that no description of the Dart Valley would be complete without the inclusion of humorous anecdotes, folklore and local legends selected from my favourite tales of the riverbank!

Mike Holgate
September 1998

A youngster in a sou'wester enjoys a trip up the Dart in 1923. Tourist guides describing the interesting sights to be seen during the eleven-mile pleasure cruise between Dartmouth and Totnes have been published since Victorian times.

Steamer Quay, Totnes, 1923. This is a queue for the down-river steamboat trip to Dartmouth. The Mortimer Brothers founded the *Totnes Times* in 1860 and published their annual *Guide to the River Dart* from the 1870s. Dartmouth's Robert Cranford followed this example, producing his guide, *Up and Down the River Dart*, by 1890.

One
East and West Dart Rivers

Day trippers pause to admire Haytor Rock in 1902. Dartmoor is the birthplace of many Devon rivers. Emerging from a moorland bog, the streams of the East and West Dart join forces at Dartmeet. From this point the River Dart flows to the estuary at Totnes, where the navigable part of the river to the sea at Dartmouth is known as 'The English Rhine'.

Cranmere Pool, Dartmoor, c. 1900. The East Dart Head rises in a peaty bog near Cranmere Pool where, according to legend, Benjamin Gayer, a seventeenth-century mayor of Okehampton, was condemned to spend the hereafter atoning for his sins. Given the impossible task of emptying the waters of the pool with a sieve, the cunning Benjie made the receptacle watertight with a piece of sheepskin, thereby making short work of his punishment!

The Cairn at Cranmere Pool was the first Dartmoor 'letterbox', where a bottle was placed for ramblers to leave their visiting cards. Following the introduction of postcards, visitors would leave them in these moorland 'postboxes', for the next person to collect and arrange for their delivery by the Royal Mail.

"The Cairn," Cranmere Pool, Dartmoor.

James Perrott of Chagford, the celebrated Dartmoor guide who erected the cairn in 1854, pictured (on the left) in 1883.

Mr H.P. Hearder of Plymouth signs the leather-bound visitors' book, which he jointly donated with Mr H. Scott-Tucker and placed in a zinc box at the cairn in 1905.

Postbridge, now a small tourist centre, boasts the largest clapper bridge on Dartmoor. Dating from the thirteenth century, it was used by packhorses travelling from the tin mines to the stannary towns of Tavistock and Chagford. In the foreground are the remains of The Barracks – an eighteenth-century tin-smelting house.

The remains of Bellever Bridge, c. 1900. Tom White of Postbridge had a tale to tell after visiting his sweetheart, a dairymaid at Huccaby Farm. As he walked home across the moor at midnight, he came across some Dartmoor pixies near Bellever Tor, who used their powers to compel him to dance with them until dawn. Following this harrowing experience, Tom became a confirmed bachelor – 'If that's what comes of courting', he decided, 'I'll go courting no more'.

Wistmans Wood, 1900. The West Dart Head is separated from its twin by less than a mile. It then takes a southerly loop before joining up with its brother at Dartmeet. Along the way, it passes an eerie copse of stunted oak trees at Wistman's Wood, the site of an ancient Dartmoor legend. Here, the Devil, in the guise of Dewer the huntsman, rides out with his pack of spectral wisht-hounds, searching for the souls of unbaptized children. A grisly folktale concerns a drunken moor man, who was returning home from the inn when he failed to recognise the dreaded Wisht-Hunt in full cry. 'Have you had good sport?' called out the moor man to the master of the hunt, 'Why yes', laughed Dewer, tossing the man a small bundle, 'Here, share our kill!'. Thinking he had been given a tasty joint of meat, the man returned home to his wife, thinking the present would prevent her from scolding him about his inebriated state. To their horror, the couple unwrapped the bundle to discover it contained the body of their own child!

Two Bridges, c. 1900. This hamlet grew up on the miners' road from Chagford to Tavistock. On the left is Crockern Tor, where the 'Tinners Parliament', was founded in 1474. In the background, on the right, is Bellever Tor. During the 1920s, a number of apparently inexplicable road accidents occurred at Cherrybrook, on the desolate stretch of road between Two Bridges and Postbridge. A motorcyclist was killed, although his two sons survived when they were thrown out of the sidecar. They claimed that two 'hairy hands' had grabbed the handlebars. An army officer also gave the same reason for a crash he was involved in. About three years later, a woman sleeping in a caravan parked near the spot awoke to see a hairy hand clawing at the window. She made a sign of the cross and the manifestation disappeared!

Hexworthy, West Dart, 1892. This is the Forest Inn, shortly before it was replaced with the present structure. Landlord Richard Cleave is sitting beneath the pubsign, which once had the distinction of being repainted by the eminent local historian William Crossing, whose guide-books to Dartmoor are still in great demand and are constantly re-published.

Jubilee Cross at Hexworthy. The memorial was carved from Dartmoor granite and erected in 1897 to commemorate the sixtieth year of Queen Victoria's reign.

Huccaby Races, 1909. This event was hosted by landowner Robert Burnard (on the extreme left). The royal visitor, Princess Mary, studies the card, a year before becoming Queen on her husband's accession to the throne as King George V. Dart Valley steeple chase meetings at Huccaby, Dartmouth and Totnes did not survive beyond the outbreak of the Second World War. Buckfastleigh Races continued until 1977 and were successfully revived in 1998.

Two
Dartmeet, Holne and Buckfastleigh

Dartmeet, c. 1930. This is one of Devon's most popular beauty spots, where the East and West Dart merge in the heart of Dartmoor. The River Dart then begins its picturesque journey flowing thirty miles to the sea.

Dartmeet Bridge, in the background, was built in 1792 to replace the old ford and clapper bridge, where this group sit and pose for the camera in 1898.

Dartmeet, June 1998. How fashions change! One hundred years later, Philip, Wendy and Barry Harvey visit the remains of the old clapper bridge – which no longer has a central section.

Badger's Holt, taken from Dartmeet Bridge, c. 1920. This postcard was published by the proprietor of the ever-popular tea gardens. The left-hand slab on the old clapper bridge was replaced in 1888 but was displaced in 1910.

This group are enjoying a picnic at Badger's Holt during the 1920s.

Fishing at Holne Chase, a wild tract of heather and woods enclosed on three sides by the river, which doubles back in a wide loop to Holne Bridge, situated beneath the hilltop village of Holne.

Holne in the 1920s. The village is clustered around the thirteenth-century church. Monks from neighbouring Buckfast Abbey contributed towards its building costs during the reign of King John.

Holne Vicarage, 1900. This was the birthplace, in 1819, of Charles Kingsley, author of *The Water Babies* and *Westward Ho!* The house in which the family lived was rebuilt in 1832.

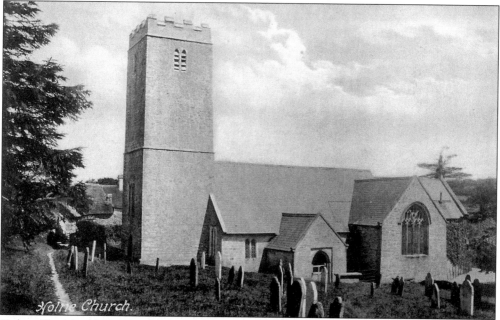

Holne Church, 1900. The font, in which Kingsley was baptised by his father in 1819, was replaced eight years later and served as a pig trough in a neighbouring farmyard until 1893. It was recovered and reinstated in the church, which contains a memorial window to Charles Kingsley.

Venford Reservoir, Holne Moor. Construction of a dam to supply Paignton with water commenced in 1901. The water engineer in charge was Frederick Vanstone, a kinsman of Isambard Kingdom Brunel.

Building materials were delivered to Buckfastleigh railway station, then transported to the site by steam traction engines. On a windy day in April 1907, sparks from an engine's funnel set fire to the thatched roofs of several cottages in the village. By the time the horse-drawn fire brigade had been summoned from Buckfastleigh, four families had been made homeless!

AT HOLNE MOOR WATERWORKS
JUNE 26 1907

Venford Reservoir was officially opened by Frederick Leyland-Barrett MP, on 26 June 1907. The road over the dam had been completed a month earlier.

Children at Holne School were given the day off to attend this special occasion with their families.

Buckfastleigh parish church. This is the burial place of the wicked squire, Richard Cabell. He was said to have sold his soul to the Devil and, following his death in 1677, locals swore that his tomb was surrounded by the howling black dogs of the Wisht-Hunt. It was this legend that inspired Arthur Conan Doyle to write the Sherlock Holmes thriller *The Hound of the Baskervilles*.

Buckfastleigh in the 1930s. To the left of the Abbey is the Higher Mills woollen factory. This was owned by the Hamlyn family until 1922, when it became a woollen store and, later, a plating works. In 1989, it was bought by Buckfast Abbey. In the background on the right is the Lower Mills woollen factory, the chimney of which was demolished in 1979. Opened by John Berry in 1850, it manufactured blankets and, later, supplied the Admiralty with serge for uniforms during both world wars. In 1950, the mill became a subsidiary of Axminster Carpets Ltd.

Three
Staverton, Dartington and Totnes

Staverton Bridge Mill, 1950. The distinctive seven arches cross the Dart where there was a corn-mill for many centuries up until the 1920s, when it was purchased by the Dartington Trust, who established Staverton Builders Ltd. While crossing the bridge in 1436, a curate of Staverton, John Laa, was attacked by one of his parishioners and retaliated – stabbing his assailant and mortally wounding him!

STAVERTON CHURCH, DEVON.

The affrighted Miller & Ventriloquist (a Midnight Adventure) E Diot

Church of St Paul de Leon. This is an 1840s postcard which, on the reverse, recounts the tale of the Miller and the Ventriloquist, which occurred when a Staverton miller met a man from Totnes who had spent the day fishing on the Dart…

The pair spent a convivial evening drinking at the Church House Inn (now the Sea Trout Inn) and walked through the churchyard at midnight, where the miller pointed out the grave of a deceased friend. The Totnesian boasted that he could communicate with the dead: 'How are you?' he enquired. 'Pretty well, thank you sur' replied a voice that seemed to come from the tomb. The terrified miller fled, leaving his companion, an accomplished ventriloquist, convulsed with laughter!

Hoode Faire, 1978. For one weekend in June, ten acres of farmland near Staverton are transformed into a scene of medieval pageantry. Revellers dress up in costume and buy home-made food and handicrafts to raise money for charity. Entertainment is provided by jesters, acrobats, magicians and musicians. In 1977, the owner of the farm, Jack Connabear, surprised everybody when his entry won the cockfight. This was a result that had seemed odds against when the 'rooster' laid an egg during the preliminaries!

James Froude (1818-1894). Destined to become one of England's great historians, Froude was born at Dartington Rectory and educated at Buckfastleigh. By the age of eleven, he was reading Homer's *Odyssey* and the *Iliad* in the original Greek. His writing reflects the historical importance of the great men of Devon and his love of the county. However, not all of his memories of home were pleasant. His elder brother bullied him as a child and he was often mercilessly thrown into the depths of the Dart!

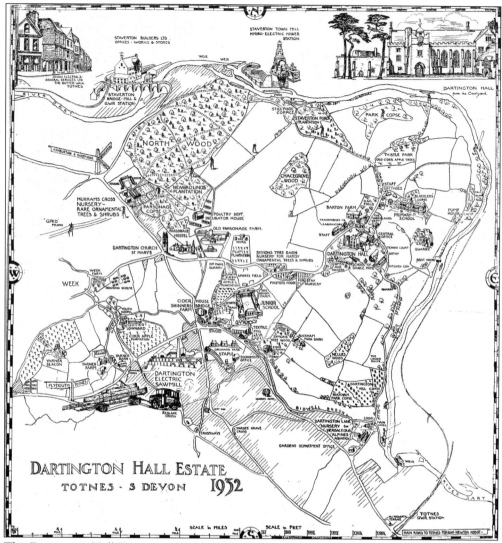

DARTINGTON HALL ESTATE
TOTNES · S DEVON 1932

The Dartington Hall Trust was established by the Elmhirst family, who took over the estate from the Champernowne family in 1925. They successfully developed ancillary industries alongside the natural agricultural resources and founded an internationally renowned arts centre for students of music, dance, drama and design.

Dartington Hall was originally built in 1392 for John Holland, the half-brother of Richard II. In 1554, the estate came into the possession of Admiral Arthur Champernowne, whose sister Katherine married twice, giving birth to four Elizabethan knights: Adrian, John and Humphrey Gilbert and their half-brother, Walter Raleigh.

A 1950s tournament of ancient sports, held at the medieval tilt-yard once used by the celebrated jouster John Holland, who was beheaded for conspiring against Henry IV.

The Great Hall, pictured soon after restoration was completed in the late 1930s. The banqueting hall had been a roofless ruin since 1814 and was expertly reconstructed by local craftsman under the supervision of the architect William Weir.

Ye Olde Cott Inne, Dartington, now known simply as the Cott Inn. It takes its name from a Dutchman, Jonas Cott, who converted the original cottages into a staging post for shepherds and sheep on their way to Totnes. Established as a public house in 1320, it is reputed to be the second-oldest inn in England.

'The good town of Totnes' – a phrase coined from author Daniel Defoe's observations during his visit in 1720. Crossing the Dart is Totnes Bridge, which opened in 1828. This replaced a wooden structure dating from the reign of King John, who had granted a charter to allow the town's affairs to be administered by the Guild of Merchants in 1206.

Totnes, c. 1890. Set in the pavement on the right-hand side, above 51 Fore Street, is the Brutus Stone. It is from this spot that the Mayor of Totnes proclaims each successive monarch to the throne. Geoffrey of Monmouthshire's twelfth-century account relates the story of the Trojan prince, Brutus, the legendary founder of Britain, who first stepped ashore on this granite rock and uttered the immortal words 'Here I sit and here I rest, this place shall be called Totnes'.

The Guildhall, 1908. Totnes is one of the oldest boroughs in England, returning its first Member of Parliament in 1295 and appointing its first mayor in 1359. In 1553, Edward VI granted a charter to convert an old priory into a guildhall, prison and 'other buildings to be used for teaching and instructing boys'. The school evolved into King Edward VI Grammar School, which survived on this site until 1887. It was then relocated to The Mansion in Fore Street and the old building was demolished and replaced by a police station.

East Gate, one of the restored medieval entrances to the town. Horse-drawn vehicles are passing under the archway into High Street. This photograph was taken soon after a new clock was installed, which struck its first hour at noon on 9 August 1880.

The Butterwalk, High Street, 1896. The piazza acquired its name when dairy produce was brought in from the agricultural areas in the South Hams and sold under the covered walkway on market day.

'The Narrows' in High Street is where the town's West Gate once stood. This bottleneck was named by stagecoach drivers, who found it to be the narrowest part of the road on the route to London. Doubtless the drivers of these 1920s vehicles agreed with their verdict!

From 1828, a toll was charged to cross Totnes Bridge. When the powers of the Turnpike Trust expired, at midnight on 1 November 1881, the townsfolk held a torchlight procession and set fire to the gates!

Totnes Bridge, 1910. A farmer drives his sheep from the livestock market towards Bridgetown, which joined the borough in 1834. The new parliamentary franchise allowed rent payers to vote, therefore the Eleventh Duke of Somerset, Edward Augustus Seymour, developed housing in the area for working-class tenants, who felt obligated to support their noble landlord's nominee at open ballot elections.

The Wills Memorial, The Plains, Totnes. The granite obelisk was erected facing the Seven Stars Hotel in 1864 and records the achievement of a Totnesian born in 1834: 'In honour of William John Wills, native of Totnes, the first with Burke to cross Australia; he perished in returning 28 June 1861'.

Totnes Carnival, 1951. Leading the floral dance is Miss Paddy Steele, crowned Queen of the Carnival by her partner, Mayor C.S. Jacka.

Totnes, The Island.

Totnes was twinned with Vire in 1971. The Island, first opened as a pleasure park in 1844, was renamed Vire Island to honour the Normandy town. As a symbol of their growing friendship, a tree-planting ceremony took place on the island in November 1978, using the same spade once used by Queen Elizabeth for a similar purpose at Dartmouth over twenty years earlier.

LITTLE HEMPSTON

Little Hempston, Totnes c. 1900. A little girl plays with her skipping rope outside the fifteenth-century church. Close by, a small tributary, the Hems, meets up with Gatcombe Brook, before they flow into the Dart half-a-mile away.

Four
Ashprington, Tuckenhay and Cornworthy

Totnes from the Sharpham Road, c. 1900. The River Dart becomes a navigable estuary from this point. A ferry from Dartmouth can be seen, carrying passengers up-river to Steamer Quay, passing a schooner moored at Mill Tail. The vessel is delivering timber from Scandanavia, imported by Francis John Reeves who began this trade in 1895.

Sharpham House, 1884. This building was designed by Sir Robert Taylor, the eminent architect, in 1770. Rivermen on passing pleasure-craft dubbed it Calendar House, erroneously telling passengers it contained 365 windows, fifty-two rooms, twelve corridors, seven entrance doors and four chimney stacks!

Sharpham, 1865. A photographer sets up his equipment on the riverbank, while the hired boatman secures his craft.

The owner of Sharpham House was considered Lord of the Manor and depended on the hilltop village of Ashprington for servants.

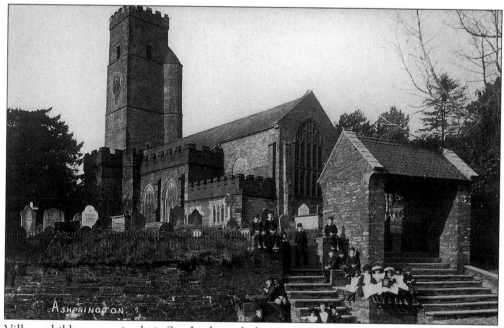

Village children pose in their Sunday-best clothes in 1905. Ashprington church tower dates from 1350 and its chalice from even earlier, being the oldest still in use in any English parish church.

Tuckenhay Paper Mill, 1915. First produced here in 1829, handmade paper was supplied for mounting the stamp collection of George VI and the proclamation of the coronation of Elizabeth II. The factory closed in 1970.

Rags being unloaded at a mill storehouse, before being made into pulp for the papermaking process.

The Waterman's Arms, Bow Bridge, Tuckenhay. In the 1920s, a Mrs Andrews, known locally as 'Lady Dora', was in the habit of calling at the hostelry in her donkey trap. Charlie the donkey was always treated to a dish of ale, which often rendered him incapable of continuing their journey. One day, a character named 'Scratchy' Skedgwell helped the animal along his way by pressing a piece of blackthorn under his tail. There was no holding Charlie as he swayed along the road pulling his mistress to Cornworthy!

Cornworthy, named for its cereal growing, has been a farming community since Saxon times. However, following the Norman Conquest, villagers had to take advantage of their proximity to Bow Creek, as they were required to render a substantial payment of fish to the Lord of Totnes.

Cornworthy, c. 1890. Traditional crafts, once used to build wooden manor houses and men-o'-war, are preserved by a local firm rejoicing in the name of Carpenter Oak and Woodland, who restored the timber roof of the medieval kitchen in Windsor Castle, destroyed in the fire of 1992.

St Peter's church dates from the fifteenth century. Standing in the shadow of the church is the schoolhouse, which was also attended by children from the neighbouring village of Tuckenhay.

Five
Stoke Gabriel, Galmpton and Dittisham

STOKE GABRIEL. 28812.

For centuries, Stoke Gabriel has been the centre of the Dart's salmon-fishing industry. It has been said that 'Salmon has for the men of the village a compulsion almost as strong as the spawning urge for the fish'.

Duncannon Quay, in the parish of Stoke Gabriel, c. 1930. A ferry service operated between Duncannon and Ashprington Point until the outbreak of the Second World War. The ferryman, tending to his boat on the left, is a member of the Hammick family who, for three generations, were summoned by passengers calling 'Boat ahoy!'

Stoke Gabriel church, where the parishioners are said to have hanged their vicar from the church tower during the reign of Queen Anne. This huge yew tree in the churchyard is thought to be at least 1,000 years old and an ancient custom has grown with it: 'Walk ye backwards round me seven times for all to see, stumble not, and then for certain one true wish will come to thee'.

Villagers at Stoke Gabriel, 1909. In keeping with Edwardian fashion, the child holding a toy rifle in the doorway of the post office – attired in boots, bonnet and dress – is a boy!

Formed in 1964, The Dartbeats were Stoke Gabriel's answer to the Merseybeat sound in the Swinging Sixties. The original line-up featured, from left to right: Roger Ball, Ray Tucker, Keith Collings, Tony Baker and Pat Baker. The group disbanded in the early 1970s, but made a remarkable comeback in 1993, which led to an appearance in a television commercial for the National Lottery (that also featured pop singer Alvin Stardust).

Greenway House is a Georgian mansion below Galmpton, overlooking the River Dart. Sir Humphrey Gilbert was born in an earlier house on the site in 1539. When the Paignton to Kingswear railway was being built, Greenway's owner, Richard Harvey, refused permission to cross the Dart with a bridge to Dittisham, which would have allowed trains to run through the South Hams to Plymouth. From 1938 until her death in 1976, the property was owned by Agatha Christie, the world-famous writer of detective fiction.

Motor launches were produced for the Royal Navy at Galmpton Creek by Stan Hall during the Second World War. In 1946, the Edhouse family converted four of these craft and launched the Western Lady Ferry Service in Torbay and organised cruises on the River Dart. The fleet is laid up at the creek during the winter months, at the company's base in the Dolphin Yacht Yard.

Galmpton's first post office was sited along The Roundings and is pictured here in 1914. A letter was once sent by a resident of Christmas Island to buy a property in the village, which the purchaser appropriately named Post Cottage.

Jubilee Tree, Galmpton, 1909. The oak tree was planted to commemorate Queen Victoria's Diamond Jubilee in 1897.

Dittisham from Greenway, 1898. In the foreground is the *Sealark*, skippered by W.G. Giles of Dartmouth.

River Dart at Dittisham.

Dittisham fishermen developed a unique solution for dealing with nagging wives. A husband would maroon his spouse in the middle of the river on the Anchor Stone, known to troubled married couples as Scold's Stone, before rowing to her rescue when the rising tide had taught her some humility!

The Dittisham Ferry, 1888. The donkey was a regular passenger to Greenway, where it was used to pull a cart carrying baskets of cockles through Galmpton to Brixham market. The human passengers sitting in the boat are: Mary Clements, her daughter-in-law, Elizabeth, and her granddaughter, Jane.

Greenway Ferry in the late 1930s. The ferry pontoon (seen in the distance on the left) was propelled by a motorboat and equipped to carry vehicles. The service has since reverted to passengers only, who still summon the boatman from Dittisham by ringing the bell. The profusion of notice boards include a table of ferry tolls, a Western National bus timetable and a blackboard for chalking up the times of steamer trips along the Dart.

Dittisham Hill with the tower of St George's church, dedicated in 1333. The road descends to the river, passing the schoolhouse, the Red Lion Inn and the village post office.

Mary Tozer talks to Fred Barrett and Miss Barrett in 1898. Both ladies served as postmistresses of Dittisham.

Six
Dartmouth and Kingswear

An aerial view of Dartmouth and Kingswear, 1930. Carved into the west bank of the Dart, the town of Dartmouth (on the left) was granted a charter by Edward III in 1341. On the opposite bank, the village of Kingswear has an even longer history. Betwixt moor and sea there are several bridges crossing the Dart, although, amazingly, these neighbours at the mouth of the river have never been linked by such a structure. An engineer, James Rendell, designed a suspension bridge in 1828, but this was opposed by local people.

OLD MILL CREEK, RIVER DART.

5200.

Dartmouth, Old Mill Creek, *c.* 1900. This is an inlet near the Britannia Royal Naval College. On the opposite bank are the remains of kilns, which used to produce lime for builders' mortar and fertiliser. In 1856, a large whale swam up the creek and became stranded when the tide receded. Local fishermen caught it and sold it for exhibition.

Castle in the Woods, Dartmouth.

15285.

At the head of Old Mill Creek stands Hermitage Castle, known locally as 'The Castle in the Wood'. The folly was built by Sir John Henry Seale of Mount Boone, who was High Sheriff of Devon in 1794.

The Butterwalk, Dartmouth, *c.* 1900. Completed in 1640 as four private dwellings, before conversion to shops, the building is considered to be one of the finest examples of seventeenth-century domestic architecture in Devon. Scammell's tobacconist's was once the home of the Dartmouth mayor, Emmanuel Wolley, who entertained Charles II here in 1671. This was the first occasion an English king had visited the town since Edward I in 1286.

Dartmouth Quay, 1865. The line of houses on the quay were completed in 1639. Two of them were later converted into the New Inn, later renamed the Castle Hotel (now the Royal Castle). The hotel is famous for its ghostly tales! Each November, the coach of Mary, consort of William III, is apparently heard re-enacting the occasion in 1689 when she was taken from her accommodation to meet her husband in Torbay!

Swans in the Boat Float. Locals remember with affection the story of Snowy the duck, who made his home here with a flock of swans. Unlike the hero of Hans Christian Anderson's tale *The Ugly Duckling*, Snowy had no inferiority complex. He mingled with the flock in the mistaken belief that he was a natural-born swan!

Dartmouth Royal Regatta, 1907. The Boat Float opened in 1882 and provided a natural pool for the annual swimming races.

Oldrieve's butchers, Dartmouth *c.* 1900. Christmas turkeys were traditionally hung above the shop to keep them fresh. Members of staff stood guard on the poultry to prevent overnight theft. The business is now a cafe on the corner of Fairfax Place and Smith Street, which is the earliest recorded thoroughfare in the town.

Knuckey's Saddlers, Lake Street, Dartmouth, *c.* 1900. When horsepower reigned supreme, every town and village had a specialist supplier of saddles, collars and harnesses for working horses. Here, Mr S.L. Smith holds a dappled grey watched by Mr Cawdell on the left.

Charabancs – the working man's motor car – became popular after the First World War. A group of trippers are preparing to leave Dartmouth Quay.

From 1920 onwards, charabancs were fitted with pneumatic tyres, a step forward in passenger comfort. During the same year, the Chief Constable of Devon and Cornwall issued a warning to charabanc drivers about the dangers of exceeding the 12 mph speed limit!

The Floating Bridge, Higher Ferry, Dartmouth, 1960. Until his death in 1965, BBC Television presenter Richard Dimbleby regularly spent his holidays at Dittisham. The popular celebrity was once embarrassed when he failed to put his handbrake on and his Rolls-Royce slipped off the back of the Higher Ferry while he was strolling on deck. The vehicle had to be recovered from the waters of the Dart!

A view of Dartmouth in the 1930s, from Church Hill, Kingswear.

The Square, Kingswear, 1915. The Royal Yacht Club Hotel was built on the site of the Plume of Feathers, after the railway reached Kingswear in 1864, then was later renamed the Royal Dart Hotel. The archway is the entrance to the Lower Ferry. On the left is Heal's general store, next door to the old post office.

Three ladies sun themselves on Lighthouse Beach in 1920. The 125-year-old Kingswear Lighthouse was demolished and replaced in 1980. A plan to reassemble it in Dartmouth's Coronation Park was scrapped when financial considerations overruled popular sentiment. James Douglass, designer of the Eddystone Lighthouse in 1882, lies buried in the graveyard of Kingswear Parish church.

The Velshada, owned by Woolworth's chairman, W.F. Stephenson, anchored by Dartmouth Castle in 1935. With an overall length of 120 feet and masts over 160 feet high, the giant J-Class yachts were a popular attraction between 1930 and 1937 when, traditionally, the last races of the season were held during the Dartmouth Regatta.

Only ten J-Class yachts were built for an exclusive club of racing millionaires, including King George V, sewing machine magnate Sir Mortimer Singer and aeroplane manufacturer Tommy Sopwith, seen here at the helm of *Endeavor* during the 1934 Torbay Royal Regatta, which always included races at Dartmouth.

Dartmouth Royal Regatta, 1935. Festooned vessels gather for the annual event, first organised in 1834. Queen Victoria donated a £25 prize during a visit in August 1856 – giving the royal assent to the occasion.

The Red Arrows made the first of their annual appearances at Dartmouth Regatta in 1978. The Gnats swooped so low over the water and the surrounding countryside that one Kingswear farmer dryly commented that 'There's no need to get the combined harvester out this year, the Red Arrows have done the job for me!'

Seven

Buckfast Abbey

Buckfast Abbey and Dartmoor, 1930. The abbey is a twentieth-century testament of faith. Benedictine monks overcame many obstacles during the re-building project, which took thirty-two years to accomplish. Starting with £5 in the kitty and a supply of sand from a local farmer, this place of worship was constructed by the monks themselves. This extraordinary feat captured the imagination of the country and donations were made by people of all denominations.

Founded in 1018 by Benedictine monks, the Abbey was reconstructed by Ethelred de Pomeroy in 1197, then occupied by Cistercians. The abbey fell into ruin following the dissolution of the monasteries by Henry VIII in 1539. Stone from the building was used to erect the neo-Gothic mansion for local mill owner Samuel Berry in 1806 (above).

In 1882, a group of Benedictine monks, driven out of France during the revolution, accepted favourable terms to purchase the site and settled at Buckfastleigh, drawn by the peace and sanctity of the location on the banks of the River Dart.

Father Boniface Natter was elected the first Abbot since the Reformation when the community was awarded abbey status in 1902. Inspired by the idea of restoring the building to its former glory, he was tragically drowned off the coast of Spain during a voyage to a mission in South America. His companion, Dom Anscar Vonier, survived the shipwreck and became Abbot, dedicating the task of rebuilding the Abbey to the memory of his predecessor. The dream was realised in 1938 and Abbot Vonier died a few weeks later on Boxing Day.

This flotilla, reminiscent of the home-made vessels that now raise money for charity in the annual Dart Raft Race, assembled on the Weir Pool during a summer bazaar in 1903. Abbot Natter is holding the flag in the leading boat, built from cider barrels by the oarsman, John Beard of Northwood Farm. The gentlemen are accompanied in the craft by Mrs Beard (on the left) and Miss Fifine Herring-Mason, a professional singer engaged to appear at the event.

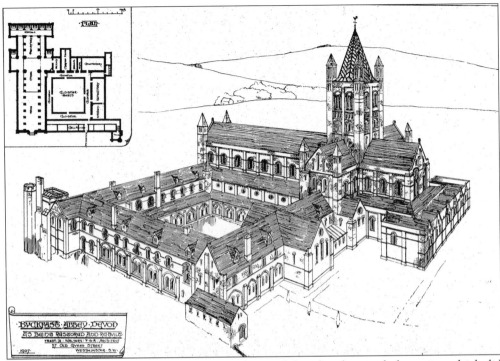

Eminent church architect Frederick Walters designed this church to include a spire, which did not materialise. Walters died in 1932 and his work was continued by his son Edward.

The first stone was laid on 5 January 1907 and the painstaking work of rebuilding the Abbey church on its medieval foundations was undertaken by the monks themselves. When the plans were first submitted to Buckfastleigh Urban District Council, one member asked the pertinent question, 'Do these monks know how to mix mortar?'

The work was supervised by Brother Peter Schrode (centre), who was sent to France to learn the craft of masonry. He, in turn, trained the brethren to assist him. Pictured here in 1925, he is accompanied by Father Richard (left) and Brother Paschal.

Usually, no more than four monks laboured on the Abbey building work. Brothers Ignatius, Peter, Paschal and Conrad are seen here in 1929, capping the tower turrets above the entrance to the church on the West Front.

Buckfast Abbey Bells.

In 1910, a peal of bells, paid for by the generosity of Sir Robert Harvey of Dunbridge, were blessed. Twelve bells were ordered and two more donated by the bell-founders. These were semi-tone bells called 'Paul' and 'Bernard', which enabled the playing of three scales instead of two. The bells were hung in the old Abbot's tower until the new belfry was completed.

Buckfast Abbey Church, (seen from the River Dart).

The Abbey rising above the bank of the Dart in 1929.

Translation of Statue of O.L. of Buckfast to the New Shrine.
August 2nd 1922.

Translation of the statue of Our Lady of Buckfast to the new shrine, 2 August 1922. The partially completed Abbey church was inaugurated for worship by the Archbishop of Westminster, Cardinal Bourne, who returned ten years later to read the address at the consecration ceremony. The statue of Our Lady with the Divine Child was destroyed during the reign of Edward VI, but a large fragment was recovered by the monks in 1884 and, from this, the whole statue was restored.

The interior of the new church crowded with worshippers.

GENERAL VIEW, BUCKFAST ABBEY.

The main tower under construction in 1930.

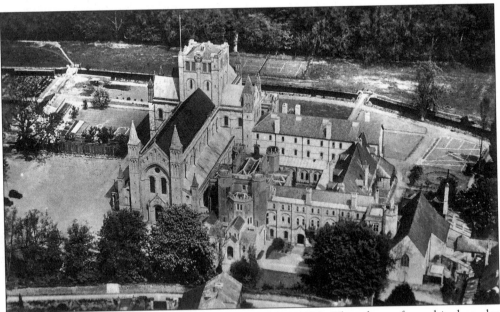

Buckfast Abbey, photographed from the air in May 1933. The place of worship has also developed into Devon's most popular tourist centre and it attracts half a million visitors a year. People flock to buy the monks' famous tonic wine and sweets made with honey from their own hives. The apiary was supervised for over half a century by the internationally renowned Brother Adam Kerhle, who died in 1996 at the age of ninety-eight. His work with bees was compared to the pioneering underwater exploration of Jacques Cousteau.

Eight
A Seafaring Tradition

Greenway House, Galmpton was the birthplace of Sir Humphrey Gilbert, the Elizabethan explorer. His half-brother, Sir Walter Raleigh, is said to have enjoyed his first pipe in England there: legend has it that his servant, seeing the burning tobacco, threw a jug of ale in his master's face to put out the fire! In 1550, John Davis was born at Sandridge in the parish of Stoke Gabriel. The navigator set sail from Dartmouth in search of the North West Passage. Before his death at the hands of Japanese pirates in 1605, the seafarer was betrayed by his Dittisham-born wife, Faith Fulford, whose lover had Davis arrested on a trumped-up charge. He was cleared by the intervention of his great friend Walter Raleigh.

A postcard commemorating Humphrey Gilbert – 'The Father of Colonisation' – who claimed Newfoundland for the Crown in 1583, but lost three of his five ships on the outward journey. Forced to return with the survivors, his own vessel, the *Squirrel*, foundered and sank off the Azores. Gilbert was last seen on deck, calmly reading a book and reassuring his crew as the storm grew worse, saying, 'We are as near to heaven by sea as by land'.

Raleigh Gilbert, Humphrey's son, inherited Compton Castle upon the death of his older brother in 1608. News of his bereavement reached him in the New World as he attempted to establish a colony on the coast of Maine. The venture was abandoned within a year, following a severe winter which brought about the deaths of many of the 120 settlers. An inscription at the landing site on the Kennebec River records his achievement: 'The first colony on the shores of New England was founded here August 19, 1607'.

Kittery Court, Kingswear. Francis Champernowne of Dartington Hall emulated the feats of his illustrious ancestors, Gilbert and Raleigh, when he sailed for America in 1636 and founded the settlement of Kittery, Maine. The township was named after another family estate in Kingswear, which his father had mortgaged to finance the venture.

Bayards Cove, where a plaque commemorates the ten-day visit of the Pilgrim Fathers on their journey to America in 1620. The *Mayflower* was accompanied by the *Speedwell*, which underwent repairs at Dartmouth. After putting to sea, the *Speedwell* began to founder and was abandoned at Plymouth before the *Mayflower* continued her epic voyage to colonise the New World.

River Dart, Sharpham, Totnes

Sharpham House. The original Elizabethan house was demolished and rebuilt for Lieutenant Philemon Pownoll, commander of HMS *Favourite*, who paid for the mansion with his share of the treasure taken from a Spanish galleon off Cadiz in 1762. Killed in action in 1780, the property passed to his daughter, who eloped to Gretna Green with Edmund Bastard. Their son John, a Member of Parliament, later lost the property when he gambled away the family fortune.

Continental trading schooners at Totnes Quay, 1865. For centuries, Totnes exported Dartmoor granite, tin, wool, cloth, leather and cider. Local shipyards produced galleons for Drake's historic defence against the Spanish Armada.

Galmpton Creek, 1935. Boatyards have been sited either side of the creek for over four centuries. Early shipbuilders included such names as Harvey and Sanders. William Gibbs ran the boatyard from 1880 and built wooden sailing trawlers for the Brixham fishing fleet. Sandstone was also brought here to be loaded onto barges, including that used to build the tower of St Mary's church, Totnes, in 1449.

The *Venture*, a tugboat, 1910. The ex-foreman of Kelly's shipbuilders, George Philip, took over his former employer's yard at Sandquay, Dartmouth, in 1858 and the company moved to their present Kingswear site at Noss Creek during the First World War. The company produced coasters, tugs, lightships and naval vessels. The yacht *British Steel* was built here for Chay Blyth's single-handed circumnavigation of the world in 1971. The Kingswear-based yachtsman's feat was later matched by another local resident, Naomi James, whose record-breaking voyage ended when she returned to Dartmouth in June 1978.

LINER LEAVING DARTMOUTH HARBOUR.
DARTMOUTH CASTLE & LIGHTHOUSE.

A liner passing Dartmouth Castle in 1905. By 1882, five ocean-going steamship companies were operating a passenger service from Dartmouth and Kingswear, travelling to all corners of the globe, including America, South Africa, the West Indies and the Falklands.

Survivors of the crew of the doomed *Titanic* leave Devonport Dockyard after returning to Plymouth on 28 April 1912. In the centre is Able Seaman J. McGough of Duncannon. Less fortunate was the ship's fireman, W. Jarvis, who never saw his Dartmouth home again!

74

Dart steamers and ferries have proudly borne the name 'Hauley' since 1877. The nomenclature commemorates a fourteenth-century privateer, John Hauley (often spelt Hawley), who plundered French merchant shipping in the Channel, with the blessing of Richard II. This enterprise made him Dartmouth's wealthiest citizen and he was elected mayor fourteen times and also represented the town in Parliament. In 1373, Geoffrey Chaucer worked as a customs officer in Dartmouth. Later, when he came to write *The Canterbury Tales*, he based the character of 'The Shipman' on his acquaintance with Hauley. Two motor tugs, *Hauley I* and *Hauley II*, were built by Philips during the 1930s, to handle the vehicle pontoon of the Dartmouth to Kingswear lower ferry, pictured above in 1949. One of the passengers waiting to board the ferry is an officer from Britannia Royal Naval College – 'The Cradle of the British Navy'.

HMS *Britannia* and *Hindustan* arrived at Dartmouth in 1863 to provide training ships for officers, including several princes of the realm. *Britannia* was replaced in 1869 by the *Prince of Wales* (centre), which took her name. In 1898, land on Mount Boone (in the background) was obtained by the Admiralty and plans approved for a shore-based college to replace the vessels. In 1905, the *Hindustan* (right) was towed to Plymouth where she was used for training until 1921. The *Britannia* became a rotting hulk and was taken to a ship-breaker in Blyth on 5 July 1916. The whole college assembled and cheered as the vessel made her final journey down the Dart. Copper from her hull was used to produce munitions for the war effort. Wood from the ship was later purchased by Agatha Christie as a souvenir and it was carved and installed in her library at Greenway.

Queen Victoria's Diamond Jubilee 1897. Officers and cadets 'splice the main brace' on board the training ship *Britannia*.

On 7 March 1902, King Edward VII laid the foundation stone for the Britannia Royal Naval College, a 'stone frigate' which opened on 14 September 1905. The design, by Sir Aston Webb, did not meet with universal approval and was described by one critic as 'hideous', resembling 'a combination of a workhouse and a stable'.

The Royal Family at Dartmouth in 1939. King George VI and Queen Elizabeth are with their daughters, Princess Margaret Rose and Princess Elizabeth. During this visit, the fourteen-year-old heir apparent met naval cadet Prince Philip for the first time and the couple were married in 1947.

Britannia Royal Naval College, 2 April 1951. Princess Margaret, followed by the college commander, Captain Dickinson, walks past the figurehead of the *Britannia* training ship, which was moored on the Dart from 1863 until 1869.

Britannia Royal Naval College, celebrating its fiftieth anniversary in 1955. The college was granted the freedom of the borough. This honour entitles members of the college, on ceremonial occasions, to 'march through the streets with bayonets fixed, drums beating and bands playing'.

Britannia Royal Naval College, July 1965. The Admiral of the Fleet, Earl Mountbatten, enjoys a joke and a cup of tea after the end of term passing out ceremony, at which he presented successful cadets with the Queen's sword, gold medal and telescopes. Two years earlier, the Earl had officiated at the opening of building extensions which were utilised as the nerve centre for his brainchild UNISON, the great Commonwealth inter-service exercise.

A time-honoured tradition enacted each Yuletide beneath a hand-steering wheel from the yacht of King Edward VII. The wife of HMS *Britannia*'s captain mixes the Christmas Pudding with an oar while the head cook adds liberal amounts of Guinness and Navy Rum!

Nine
A History of Warfare

The mouth of the Dart was defended in medieval times by two castles. Dartmouth Castle dates from 1481, replacing a fortification built in 1388. Kingswear Castle, on the opposite bank, was built ten years later near the ruins of Godmerock Fort. A chain stretched across the water, called 'Old Jawbones', provided an ingenious deterrent to enemy ships. A new improved version of the chain was introduced during the Second World War to keep out U-boats.

Dartmouth from above Warfleet.

Warfleet Creek, at the mouth of the Dart, where fleets of warships have gathered since the Middle Ages. Vessels assembled here for Richard the Lionheart's crusade in 1190. In 1346, a force joined Edward III for the siege of Calais, while another fleet sailed twenty years later for Gascony. The anchorage was used at the time of the Armada in 1588.

The memorial tablet on the quay, unveiled by the Duke of Edinburgh on 12 July 1954. This commemorates the force of 480 British and American craft which left Dartmouth to take part in the D-Day landings in June 1944.

Dartmouth and Kingswear supported the Parliamentarians during the Civil War, but fell to Prince Maurice after a month's siege in 1643. Sir Edward Seymour of Berry Pomeroy was appointed Royalist governor of Dartmouth, while Henry Cary of Cockington held Kingswear. Three years later, both garrisons surrendered to the Roundheads commanded by Thomas Fairfax.

Kingswear Castle (in the foreground) was abandoned after the Civil War, until restored by prominent politician Charles Seale-Hayne in 1855. A century later, it became the home of Sir Frederick Bennett, Torbay Member of Parliament from 1955 until 1987.

Palmerston Gun Battery, pictured shortly after installation in the 1860s. Dartmouth Castle was the first castle in England to be designed to have guns as its main armament, with gun-ports covering the approach to the estuary.

Bearscove Castle at Bayards Cove, 1865. Children play in the remains of an artillery battery, created in 1537 as a part of Henry VIII's coastal defence scheme. It was adapted briefly as a machine-gun strongpoint during the Second World War.

St Petrox church existed for two centuries before the adjoining Dartmouth Castle. It was used as a provisions store during the Civil War. The names of local people who fell in the two world wars are inscribed on a memorial inside the church.

Compton Castle, c. 1900. The Gilbert family of Greenway built this inland fortification to combat the fear of invasion from the French during the 1340s. The castle was abandoned in 1800 and became an ivy-covered ruin. In 1904, Walter Raleigh Gilbert visited his ancestral home on his way to join HMS *Britannia* at Dartmouth and, in 1930, fulfilled his ambition to purchase it. Restoration was completed in 1951 and the castle was then handed over to the guardianship of the National Trust.

The Norman castle at Berry Pomeroy was occupied by only two families. The Pomeroys, who landed with William the Conqueror, and the Seymours, who purchased the property in 1548.

William of Orange landed at Brixham in 1688 and, according to traditional supposition, halted at Berry Pomeroy. When introduced to his host, William enquired, 'I think, Sir Edward, that you are of the family of the Duke of Somerset'. Seymour politely corrected his guest, 'Pardon me, your Highness, the Duke of Somerset is one of my family'.

Parliament Cottages, Longcombe, near Stoke Gabriel. William of Orange was unsure of the reception he would receive in his avowed intent to 'deliver the nation from Popery'. Remembering the failure of the Monmouth Rebellion, many nobles were reluctant to affirm their allegiance. Having been recently deposed as Recorder of Totnes by King James II, Seymour had no such qualms. He provided the prince with this farmhouse, in which to hold his first 'parliament'.

One of the ghosts of the Pomeroy family, who are said to haunt the castle, is cleverly superimposed on this postcard. This may be the reason why the castle was suddenly abandoned without explanation following the death of Edward Seymour in 1708. The building was later struck by lightning and fell into ruin.

Totnes Castle, 1904. The fortification was constructed after the Battle of Hastings. Further work was ordered by William de Zouche, one of the barons who overthrew Edward II in 1326. The Yorkist Zouches held the manor until defeat at Bosworth Field in 1485. From 1559 until 1947, it was owned by the Seymour family.

Totnes, viewed from the castle keep, with St Mary's church on the left and the estuary of the Dart on the extreme right. During the Civil War, the town supported Parliament but did not wish to take up arms against the King. Both sides occupied the town and the peace was kept by meekly submitting to the demands of both Roundheads and Royalists for money and supplies. Sick soldiers also spread the plague, which brought about the deaths of 250 local people.

North Gate, adjoining the castle, *c.* 1900. In medieval times, Totnes was enclosed by walls, with entrances at four gates. The South Gate and West (or Shambles) Gate are now non-existent.

East Gate originally had two arched openings, a large one for carriages and a 'needle's eye' that allowed pedestrians through in single file. It was rebuilt with a single arch and an inbuilt clock. The structure required extensive restoration after being totally destroyed by fire in 1990.

Totnes Castle. An Elizabethan pageant in the castle grounds, soon after the property had been acquired by the Ministry of Works in 1947.

An Iron Age fortification exists at Holne Chase, where a gamekeeper found a cache of spearheads in 1871. Between Holne and Buckfastleigh, there is another earthwork, Hembury Castle, known locally as Danes Camp. It is said that when Norsemen pillaged their way up the River Dart, they got their comeuppance when they reached Hembury. The womenfolk allowed themselves to be abducted, then slew their Danish captors when they fell asleep!

Dom Ansar Vonier. In July 1914, the Abbot of Buckfastleigh was taking a holiday in the Tyrol when Austria declared war on Serbia. He was mistakenly fired upon by a soldier who was searching for a Serbian spy and then, a few days later when Britain entered the war, he was arrested in the marketplace of Gastein and taken, under armed escort, to Saltzberg where he was held as an English spy. Cleared of this charge, he was interred for two months before representations from the Vatican secured his release and he returned to Buckfastleigh. The Abbot, like most of his fellow monks, was born in Germany and they were treated with some suspicion, requiring a special licence to travel more than five miles from the abbey.

Buckfastleigh, *c.* 1914. The army displays its firepower to the town's youngsters during a recruiting drive.

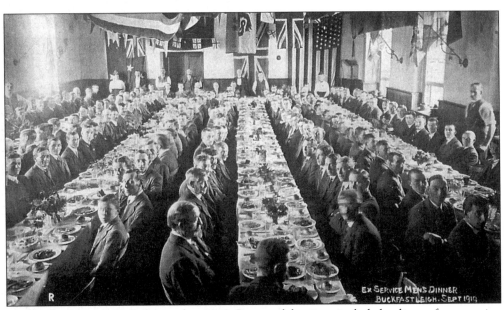

Buckfastleigh Town Hall, September 1919. Peace celebrations included a dinner for returning ex-servicemen.

The Armistice is officially announced to the crowd gathered outside St Mary's church by Totnes' mayor, C.F. Rea, on Monday 11 November 1918.

General Sir William Riddell Birdwood inspects Totnes veterans in August 1919. His forebears occupied Birdwood House (now a community centre) and, in recognition of these ancestral links with Totnes, the general became the sixth member of his family to be awarded the freedom of the borough. When raised to the peerage he became Baron Birdwood of Anzac and Totnes.

Totnes War Memorial, 1921. The unveiling ceremony at St Mary's church by General Birdwood, who had led liberation forces in France after recovering from a wound received at Gallipolli. His example in battle proved an inspiration to Australian and New Zealander soldiers, who named him 'The Soul of Anzac'.

The Prince of Wales unveiled Dartmouth's war memorial in 1921 and signed the autograph book of local hero, Corporal Theo 'Tommy' Veale. In 1916, the soldier risked his life to rescue a wounded officer from a shell hole at the Battle of the Somme. Veale was Dartmouth's first volunteer to join up and fulfilled his boastful parting to his friends, 'Goodbye, I'm off to win the Victoria Cross!'

The *Mew*, arriving at Kingswear on 25 April 1917, carrying troops from the 7th London Regiment. In May 1940, the GWR ferry, captained by Bill Harris, answered the nation's call to assist the relief of Dunkirk, but was deemed unsuitable and turned back at Dover. Her moment of glory came a year later, when she went to the rescue of the *Mistral* and helped to tow the destroyer to safety after the vessel had drifted onto rocks by Bayard's Cove, whilst turning in bad weather.

General de Gaulle inspects the Free French naval officers of the 23rd MTB flotilla, based at Kingswear during the Second World War.

The Noss shipyard of Philip & Son at Kingswear was attacked by German aircraft on 18 September 1942, resulting in the loss of twenty workers. A permanent memorial, on the site of the old shipyard near the higher ferry, was dedicated to them by the vicar of Dartmouth, John Butler, on 7 October 1988.

Duke Street, Dartmouth, 13 February 1943. Fourteen people were killed in a surprise hit-and-run raid by four German bombers, who swooped in low between the river-mouth castles. The historic Butterwalk was badly damaged but later restored.

IMPORTANT MEETINGS

The area described below is to be REQUISITIONED urgently for military purposes, and must be cleared of its inhabitants by DECEMBER 20th, 1943.

Arrangements have been made to help the people in their moves, to settle them elsewhere, and to advise and assist them in the many problems with which they will be faced. To explain these arrangements

PUBLIC MEETINGS

will be held as follows :

FRIDAY Nov. 12th

11 a.m. **EAST ALLINGTON CHURCH**

2-30 p.m. **STOKENHAM CHURCH**

Earl Fortescue, M.C., The Lord Lieutenant in the Chair.

SATURDAY Nov. 13th

11 a.m. **BLACKAWTON CHURCH**

2-30 p.m. **SLAPTON VILLAGE HALL**

Sir John Daw, J.P., Chairman Devon County Council in the Chair.

These general meetings will be immediately followed by special meetings to discuss the problems of farmers, who are requested to remain behind for them.

IT IS VITALLY IMPORTANT to every householder that he should arrange to attend whichever of these meetings is nearest to his home, and where necessary employers of labour are requested to give their work-people time off for this purpose.

THE AREA AFFECTED

ALL LAND AND BUILDINGS lying within the line from the sea at the east end of Blackpool Bay in Stoke Fleming parish to Bowden; thence northward along the road to the Sportsman's Arms; thence west along the Dittisham-Halwell road to the cross-roads ½-mile east of Halwell village; from this cross-road along the Kingsbridge road to the Woodleigh-Buckland cross-roads; thence along the road Buckland, Frogmore, Chillington, Beeson and Beesands to the sea, but excluding the villages of Frogmore, Beeson and Beesands. The roads forming the boundary are outside the area.

The parishes involved are the whole, or almost the whole, of Blackawton, East Allington, Sherford, Slapton and Strete, most of Stokenham, and parts of Stoke Fleming, Buckland-tout-Saints and Halwell.

In December 1943, 3,000 inhabitants of South Hams villages were given six weeks' notice to evacuate their homes to accommodate the influx of American troops training for the decisive Normandy landings carried out on D-Day, 6 June 1944. Most of the inhabitants moved to neighbouring towns and villages along the River Dart.

Agatha Christie (1890-1976). 'The Queen of Crime' was born in Torquay and, during the First World War, worked in an emergency war hospital for wounded Belgium soldiers. Using her knowledge of drugs, learned as a dispensary nurse, she wrote her first murder mystery introducing the Belgium detective, Hercule Poirot. In 1938, she bought Greenway House and the mansion was requisitioned to accommodate American naval officers during the Second World War. The library was used as the mess-room and one officer painted a fresco on the wall, which included portraits of the Allied leaders: Churchill, Stalin and Roosevelt. The author turned down offers from the Admiralty to restore the room and was delighted to keep her own 'war memorial'.

51456. Agatha Christie's Cottage, Dittisham-on-the-Dart.

Agatha Christie's cottage on the Greenway estate, 1945. In an autobiography published after her death, the famous crime writer recalled the terror of Messerschmidt Me109s flying low up-river, strafing civilian targets. A group of nuns and pupils, evacuated to Sharpham House from a Southsea convent school, were compelled to dive for cover as they were attacked while holding an outdoor PE class. More seriously, a schoolmistress at Cornworthy was wounded while supervising children in the playground. One German fighter pilot, shot down over Galmpton, parachuted into an orchard, where an ARP officer based at the Village Institute took him prisoner and made him a cup of tea!

An American tank beside Dartmouth's Coronation Park in 1944.

A badly damaged Landing Ship Tank is brought to Dartmouth for repair, following the disastrous Exercise Tiger. German E-Boats attacked the Americans as they practised a landing on the beach at Slapton. Over 700 Americans were drowned and further casualties resulted from 'friendly fire'. Thankfully, the hard lesson was learned and fewer troops lost their lives on D-Day.

At the outbreak of the Second World War, Dartmouth resident Vernon McAndrew, a noted helmsman who won the King's Cup at Cowes, sailing *Trivia*, offered his motor yacht, *Campeador V* to the Admiralty. Built at Philip's yard in 1938, the vessel was commissioned on 18 September 1939, but was lost with her owner and crew when she struck an enemy mine off the Isle of Wight on 22 June 1940.

Royal Naval minesweeper 1040 built at Totnes. In August 1940, yacht-builder Frank Curtis set up a boatyard for the Admiralty at Mill Tail. The workshops on the Bridgetown bank employed 600 people and produced twenty-three minesweepers and 400 barges for the Allied assault on Normandy.

An aerial view of Dartmouth, taken in 1948. On the right are the workshops of the American wartime naval repair base, on the site of Coronation Park. Concrete 'hards' are positioned at the water's edge, for the embarkation of tanks.

Britannia Royal Naval College, May 1969. The Queen Mother, escorted by Captain David Williams, is introduced to the chief cook, John Hemmings, who was severely wounded during the Second World War, while serving on the ill-fated HMS *Walney*. The ship was sunk by the Vichy French during an attempt to capture Oran Harbour in November 1942. The enemy were well prepared and most of those aboard the *Walney* lost their lives. Survivors were released from captivity a few days later by American forces. The commander of the 'suicide mission', Captain Frederick Peters, was the only one of seventeen men on the bridge to survive but, tragically, he died a few days later in a plane crash while returning to Britain on a special mission for General Eisenhower. He was posthumously awarded the Victoria Cross.

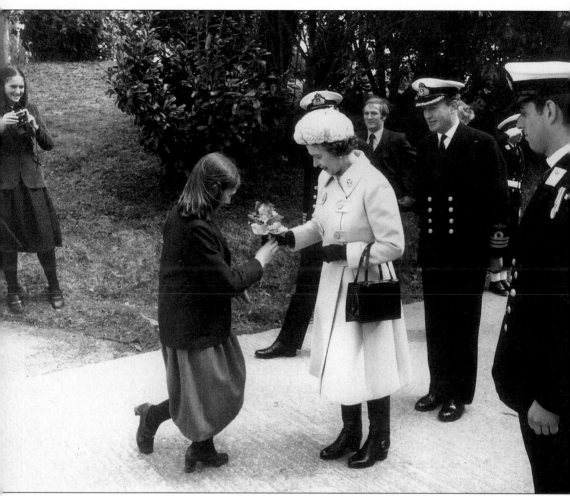

The Queen is presented with a posy at the BRNC in 1980. Her Majesty was attending the passing out ceremony of Prince Andrew. Two years later, the Prince was on active service as a helicopter pilot in the Falkland Islands. During the campaign, Colonel Herbert Jones lost his life at the Battle of Goose Green and was posthumously awarded the Victoria Cross. Born at The Grange, Kingswear, a special plaque, bearing the name of 'Colonel H', was carved in oak at Dartington and erected to the memory of people who fell in conflicts other than the two world wars. The memorial was unveiled at Kingswear Parish church by the Archdeacon of Totnes.

Ten

Steam on the Dart

The railway reached Kingswear in 1864, a year after the naval training vessels *Britannia* and *Hindustan* had arrived. Crossing the river is the floating bridge, on the site of the higher ferry.

'The Father of the Steam Engine' – Thomas Newcomen (1666-1729). The Dartmouth engineer invented the first practical working steam engine, which proved successful pumping water out of Cornish mines. James Watt later applied the principle to turn the wheel and, through the development work of engineers such as George and Robert Stephenson, the railway was born. This memorial to Dartmouth's celebrated son was unveiled in the town's public gardens by the Newcomen Society in 1929, to commemorate the bicentenary of his death. The picture was taken by professional photographer Fred Holwill, who later became Mayor of Dartmouth. His wife, Dolly, also served as mayor, becoming the first lady to be so honoured by the town in 1954.

Isambard Kingdom Brunel (1806-1859). The engineer of the Great Western Railway adapted Newcomen's atmospheric engine by building pumping stations for the South Devon Railway Company. A vacuum was created in a continuous pipe situated between the tracks drawing a piston to haul the train. The system failed due to rats gnawing through the leather valves. As a consequence, the railroad faced severe financial difficulties, which caused considerable delay in building the line from Torquay to Kingswear that commenced a year before Brunel's death.

The railroad reached Totnes in 1847, on the main route between Newton Abbot and Plymouth. The Buckfastleigh, Totnes and South Devon Railway branch line opened on 1 May 1872. Totnes Station, pictured here in 1925, features one of Brunel's old atmospheric pumping stations (on the left), which was never fitted with a steam engine. The building is now owned by Unigate Creamery.

Staverton Railway Station, between Totnes and Buckfastleigh, pictured at the turn of the century.

Railway staff at Staverton Station, 1921. They are, from left to right: Leonard Napper (lad porter), Mr Bartlett (stationmaster) and Fred Baker (signalman). A year after this photograph was taken, Fred Baker married a young booking clerk, Nellie Drennan, whose father Robert was Mayor of Totnes and editor of the *Totnes Times*.

Buckfastleigh, 1906. The noon train leaves the station, passing the stationmaster's house, at the start of the seven-mile journey beside the Dart to Totnes. The other building in the field is the Co-operative Coal Stores.

Edwardian passengers at Buckfastleigh await the arrival of the Ashburton to Totnes service.

The Dartmouth and Torbay Railway Act received the Royal Assent in 1857 and construction was officially started at Torre in January 1858. To the accompaniment of a band, a large crowd and 'bumpers of champagne and other edibles', the chairman of the railway company, Charles Seale-Hayne, caused much amusement when he broke the ceremonial spade in half whilst attempting to cut the first sod.

An early photograph of a saddle tank locomotive at Kingswear Station, which opened in August 1864. Brunel's broad gauge track was abandoned in favour of the universally accepted standard gauge in 1892.

On 21 September 1866, a train crash occured on the new line. Workmen had not completed installing a point and, with no signalling system to warn the driver, the train travelling from Kingswear to Torquay ran off the broad gauge track at Hollacombe.

The *Edyth*, moored off Philip's boatyard shortly after construction in 1872. George Parker Bidder, known in his youth as 'The Calculating Boy', was born with an amazing ability for mental arithmetic. His father, a Mortenhampstead stonemason, displayed his son's genius at fairs before wealthy gentlemen provided money for an education. After studying civil engineering at Edinburgh University, Bidder became a partner of Robert Stephenson, building railways in Britain and Europe. In 1858, he arrived at Dartmouth by yacht and resided in the town until his death in 1878. Bidder designed the steam trawler *Edyth*, which he named after his daughter.

The world's only railway station without a track opened at Dartmouth in 1889. Passengers were transferred by ferry from Kingswear to Dartmouth, where carriages waited to enable people to complete their journey. In 1917, motor vehicles replaced the horse-drawn service to Kingsbridge.

Paignton Station, 17 April 1905. This was the opening day of the Great Western Railway's bus service connecting the two South Devon branch lines between Paignton and Totnes.

Built in 1894, The *Duchess of Devonshire* paddle steamer operated combined river and coastal trips and was joined two years later by her 'sister' ship, the *Duke of Devonshire*. The vessels were designed to nose ashore on resort beaches. The *Duchess* is seen here departing from Paignton Pier in 1923.

The *Duchess of Devonshire* was wrecked when she lost her anchor and ran aground at Sidmouth in 1934. The *Duke of Devonshire* operated as a minesweeper during both world wars and survived until 1978. The paddle steamer was towed to the breakers after spending the previous two years as a floating base for sailboat holidays at Dartmouth.

The Floating Bridge, 1848. Originally steam-driven, when the ferry was introduced in 1831, it proved too costly to run, so two blind horses took over the task in 1835, operating a treadmill to pull the craft across on two chains. The floating bridge was designed by James Rendel. A commemorative plaque to the inventor was unveiled near the higher ferry by Sir John Seale in November 1988.

In 1855 the bridge broke its moorings and sank. The following year, Kelly's of Dartmouth built the ferry pictured above. It was operated from inside a box on-board the vessel, in which a horse hauled the chains by walking round a horizontal capstan.

The Floating Bridge, 1910. In 1863, steam was re-introduced, with a ferry built by Philip's of Dartmouth.

The Lower Ferry, c. 1900. Feudal landlord William Cary first introduced a ferry service on this site in 1365, which was powered by oarsmen. In 1870, a steam tug (on the left) towed the float across the river. Owned by the railway company, the ferry was leased to the Casey family from 1877 until 1925, when Dartmouth Corporation took over the operation. In October 1989, a new ferry float was introduced and named to honour the doyen of ferrymen, Tom Casey, who died in 1976 at the age of ninety-five, having spent all his life in Kingswear.

The *Dolphin* steamboat, built by Philip's, was launched in 1869 to ferry railway passengers between Kingswear and Dartmouth Stations. It was specially designed with two prows to enable it to travel in either direction, thereby saving time manoeuvring in and out of the jetties.

The Great Western Railway took over the South Devon lines in 1876 and in 1908, replacing the *Dolphin* with a twin-screw steamer, the SS *Mew*. The ferry was later converted to carry cars and stayed in service until 8 October 1954. Before being scrapped, she made her last trip across the Dart amid an emotional farewell of rockets and ships' sirens!

In 1882, John Lee worked at the Royal Yacht Club Hotel (now the Royal Dart Hotel), which provided accommodation for Great Western Railway passengers. Dissatisfied with his lowly position of boot-boy, he became a porter at Kingswear Station, before transferring to the goods department at Torre. Two years later, while working as a manservant, he received the death penalty for the brutal killing of his elderly female employer – the infamous case of the Babbacombe Murder. Mysteriously, he survived three execution attempts and the sentence was commuted to life-imprisonment. In 1894, Lee's father wrote to Charles Seale-Hayne, complaining that he was only permitted four visits a year to Portland Prison for a period of only thirty minutes and the cost was prohibitive to a man of his lowly means. He asked the MP's assistance in helping him to see his son just once a year for one hour. The letter was passed to the Home Secretary, who flatly turned down the request. Lee was eventually released in 1907 and wrote a best-selling autobiography called *The Man They Could Not Hang*!

Charles Babbage (1791-1871). The Totnes mathematical genius is remembered as The Father of the computer, through his pioneering work with the Analytical Engine. He also had a great passion for trains and was a close friend and associate of Brunel. In 1830, while attending the opening of the Manchester to Liverpool Railway, to see Stephenson's *Rocket* put through its paces, he thought of up the idea of sweeping obstacles off the track by attaching a device to the front of the engine. The concept found little support in Britain, but his invention of the 'cowcatcher' became a distinctive feature of American railroads, where trains crossing open country faced potential derailment from roaming herds of cattle or buffalo. A Babbage ambition to walk on water ended with a soaking when he tried to emulate a steamboat and cross the River Dart with paddles attached to his feet!

George Jackson Churchward (1857-1933). Born in Stoke Gabriel and educated at Totnes Grammar School, Churchward was appointed Chief Mechanical Engineer of the Great Western Railway in 1902, having starting his career as an apprentice at Newton Abbot maintenance sheds. Through his brilliant development work, he became known as the 'Father of the Modern Steam Engine'. Ironically, he was killed by a train while crossing the line near his retirement home in Swindon.

Kingswear Station, 1972. Churchward's spirit lives on along the Dart, where a few of his famous engines still run, operating on the preserved steam railways between Paignton and Dartmouth and Buckfastleigh and Totnes. The official inaugural specials, to mark the re-opening of the two lines, were pulled by No. 4555, an engine of the 4500 class introduced (by Churchward) in 1906, which had worked the last British Rail freight out of Buckfastleigh in 1962.

The locomotive turntable by the creek, pictured shortly after installation at Kingswear in 1915.

Kingswear Turntable, 1950. Crews had the strenuous task of manually turning the engine. British Rail removed the apparatus following the station's closure in the 1960s.

Kingswear, *c.* 1915. The *Ophir* steam locomotive stands in the foreground, while on the river beyond the carriage is the pontoon of the lower ferry. In the background, at the top right, are three passenger paddle steamers, owned by the River Dart Steamboat Company and named after South Devon castles. The vessels were laid up during the First World War. Nearest to the camera is the newest addition to the fleet, *Compton Castle*, built in 1914. The other two ferries are *Berry Castle* and *Dartmouth Castle*, built in 1904 and 1907 respectively. The first of the 'Castle' steamers was built by Polybanks at Kingswear in 1880, and it established a distinctive style of craft which were to grace the river until 1965.

Dartmouth Harbour mouth.

By the turn of the twentieth century, steam was fast replacing sail. A number of small steamships had operated on the Dart since 1836, with mixed success. The Dartmouth Steam Packet Company was formed in 1859 and built up a fleet of five vessels, which operated a regular service to Totnes, calling at Greenway, Dittisham and Duncannon. By 1906, this river packet and excursion service had evolved into the River Dart Steamboat Company.

Greenway Pier, soon after construction in 1922. This structure enabled passengers to be picked up at low tide. The 'Castle' steamer excursions also provided an important local transport service. People and farm produce, bound for market at Totnes or Dartmouth, would go out by small boat to await the steamers and be picked up at various points along the river – a practice that continued until the outbreak of the Second World War.

Steamer Quay, Totnes, 1907. *Totnes Castle* was built by Philip's in 1896. She was taken out of service in 1912 and converted into a houseboat.

Kingswear Castle (left) and *Compton Castle* moored at Totnes Steamer Quay in 1960. Two years later, *Compton Castle* was converted into a waterside cafe at Kingsbridge. *Kingswear Castle*, built by Philip's in 1924, was withdrawn in 1965. Britain's last coal-fired steamer was then moored up at Mill Creek, alongside the remains of her sister ship *Dartmouth Castle*, and put up for sale. It was bought and painstakingly restored by the Paddle Steamer Preservation Society. Twenty years later, it commenced operating excursions on the River Medway.

Dartmouth Castle, built by Philip's in 1948, was one of a fleet of five modern diesel-driven vessels which gradually replaced the steam-powered 'Castle' class. The River Dart Steamboat Company was taken over by Evans and Reid of Cardiff, who honoured their Welsh heritage by naming two of the boats *Cardiff Castle* and *Conway Castle*.

The *County of Brecknock* at Kingswear Station in 1960. Beyond the footbridge are the pillars supporting the recently constructed 'Banjo' – a semi-circular road widening measure on the Brixham Road. This was the year of 'The Beeching Axe', which led to the closure of many branch lines, including Paignton to Kingswear and the Totnes to Ashburton line. Fortunately, steam enthusiasts would not let them die.

A train crossing the Maypool Viaduct before entering Greenway Tunnel during the declining years of steam, May 1955.

1275. Maypool Viaduct, Nr. Dartmouth.

Staverton Railway Station, 3 November 1958. The last British Rail passenger train on the Totnes to Ashburton line. A goods service, carrying mainly cattle, continued until Friday 7 September 1962. On the following day, the Plymouth Railway Circle chartered a special train for a farewell ride up the branch to Ashburton.

Opening of the Dart Valley Railway line at Buckfastleigh, Saturday 21 May 1969. Dr Beeching (right) officiated at the ceremony and quipped, 'If I had not closed this branch, I could not now be opening it!'

Opening of the Torbay Steam Railway on New Years Eve 1972. Among the guests were the Earl of Devon, the chairman of Kingswear Parish Council, Harry Roscoe, and (pictured above) the Mayor and Mayoress of Dartmouth, Mr and Mrs Frank Mullett. Regular passenger services on the Paignton to Kingswear line were resumed the following day – on the twenty-fifth anniversary of railway nationalisation.

Acknowledgements

The majority of the photographs and illustrations used in this book were obtained from the Local Studies Archive at Torquay Library. My appreciation goes to the Torbay Reference Librarian, Anne Howard, for allowing these pictures to be used. Grateful thanks also go to all my colleagues in the 'Ref' for their continuous help and support. For additional photographs and information, I am indebited to my sister, Sandra Jackson; Ray Tucker of the Dartbeats; the Hemmings family of Brixham; Father Jerome of Buckfast Abbey; Don Collinson of Kingswear; David Mason and Ray Nickells of the Torbay Postcard Club. Lastly, the book could not have been compiled without the assistance of Wendy Harvey, whose contacts and local knowledge of the towns and villages around the Dart proved invaluable to my research.